VIOLA

**HAL•LEONARD
INSTRUMENTAL
PLAY-ALONG**

AUDIO
ACCESS
INCLUDED

PLAYBACK+
• Pitch • Balance • Loop

Disney

Aladdin

Audio arrangements by Peter Deneff

To access audio visit:
www.halleonard.com/mylibrary

Enter Code
2937-5665-1894-3834

Motion Picture Artwork TM & Copyright © 2019 Disney

ISBN 978-1-5400-6242-0

Visit Hal Leonard Online at
www.halleonard.com

Contact us:
Hal Leonard
7777 West Bluemound Road
Milwaukee, WI 53213
Email: info@halleonard.com

In Europe, contact:
Hal Leonard Europe Limited
42 Wigmore Street
Marylebone, London, W1U 2RN
Email: info@halleonardeurope.com

In Australia, contact:
Hal Leonard Australia Pty. Ltd.
4 Lentara Court
Cheltenham, Victoria, 3192 Australia
Email: info@halleonard.com.au

Contents

4

ARABIAN NIGHTS
(2019)

VIOLA

Music by ALAN MENKEN
Lyrics by HOWARD ASHMAN
BENJ PASEK and JUSTIN PAUL

ONE JUMP AHEAD

VIOLA

Music by ALAN MENKEN
Lyrics by TIM RICE

FRIEND LIKE ME

VIOLA

Music by ALAN MENKEN
Lyrics by HOWARD ASHMAN

PRINCE ALI

VIOLA

Music by ALAN MENKEN
Lyrics by HOWARD ASHMAN

Slower, accelerating gradually

SPEECHLESS

VIOLA

Music by ALAN MENKEN
Lyrics by BENJ PASEK
and JUSTIN PAUL

Moderately
Piano

A WHOLE NEW WORLD

VIOLA

Music by ALAN MENKEN
Lyrics by TIM RICE